Kassi Psifogeorgou

OUR VERY GREEK EASTER

Illustrated by
Laura Mocelin

Published by
Adventuresome Words
Buckinghamshire
England
www.adventuresomewords.co.uk
info@adventuresomewords.co.uk

First published by Adventuresome Words in 2022.
Text and illustrations copyright © Kassi Psifogeorgou. 2022.
Illustrator: Laura Mocelin.

Kassi Psifogeorgou
Our very Greek Easter
ISBN:978-1-9168989-7-4

Dedication

To all those who love Greece and plan to visit it one day.

To Nickolas, Konstantinos, Panagiotis, and Demis, the four angels in my life.

To the beautiful godparents of my children.

To my goddaughters.

To my parents.

To our wonderful friends who always travel great distances to see us.

Dear Alina,

I hope you are well and enjoying the school break.

As you know, we flew to Greece ten days ago. We've been staying in Volos where Yiayia, Papou, Thea (aunty), and our godparents live; it's sunny here all day long, getting warmer every second. We are having such a wonderful time, and I feel so lucky that mum and dad surprised us with an Easter trip this year.

My twin brother George and my younger brother John couldn't stop talking about who would meet us at the airport, what we'd eat for dinner and Greece's wonderful Easter traditions.

I'm staying true to my word and writing to you about all the fantastic things we've done. I'm so excited to tell you!

Oh! Also, it is grandpa's birthday on Easter Sunday!

You're probably thinking, "Hold your horses, Tom, and start from the beginning!" Hee hee hee! I can almost hear you yelling at me. I know; you're always right. So, let's start at the beginning.

Pascha, or Greek Orthodox Easter, is our family's most important religious holiday. Yiayia and Papou always take us to church during Holy Week and talk about our traditions. We also help prepare Easter sweets and Easter Sunday specialities!

Here is what I've learned.

The Greeks call Jesus, Christ, which means "anointed". An anointed person is someone who has been set apart for God's purposes. But grandma says that when we refer to Christ as "anointed one", we describe him as God himself.

A week-long celebration leads to Pascha. Many symbolic events happen through this Holy Week, and the whole country follows the traditions. Each day of the Holy Week has a different theme at the church. The priests read the Gospels, and we remember the events leading up to Christ's death and resurrection.

To prepare themselves for Easter, many follow the Great Lent. They don't eat meat, milk, eggs, or dairy products. This tradition always begins on Clean Monday; it lasts for forty days and ends on Holy Saturday night. Others choose to fast during Holy Week. My family practices this kind of fasting.

DAY 1. LAZARUS SATURDAY

For us, the celebrations start on the Saturday of Lazarus. According to the Gospels, Lazarus of Bethany was raised from the dead on this day. After hearing about Lazarus' death, Christ went to Bethany only four days later to bring him back from the dead. Dressed in his funeral clothes, Lazarus came out. According to Papou, this is the last great miracle Christ did before his resurrection.

Today, children go door to door singing about Lazarus, holding baskets decorated with flowers and getting treats. But unlike the old days when people gave away eggs as a gift, these days, it's mostly money. My mum told me that she used to do this when she was young and that it is a tradition that is mostly followed by girls. But there's nothing wrong with doing it if we want to. So, of course, we were eager to participate!

We made a quick map of the houses we'd go to, starting with Thea's.
We then got to make these delicious sweet and spiced Lenten biscuits. They are called Lazarakia, and they resemble Lazarus, dressed in grave clothes like he'd just risen from the dead. And guess what? We carved lips on them and used cloves for eyes!

Thea's tip: Lazarakia aren't supposed to be shiny, so avoid using egg or butter to brush them.

DAY 2. PALM SUNDAY (KIRIAKI TON VAION)

Palm Sunday marks Christ's arrival in Jerusalem and is celebrated one week before Easter. We use palms to decorate our churches because that is what people used to do in the past to show their happiness when celebrating something important!

When we went to the church, Yiayia and Papou sat us close to the altar so that we could see everything clearly. The priest blessed the palms, soaked them in holy water and sprayed everyone. Naturally, we all got wet, but it was so much fun! Then, they gave palm branches away for everyone to take home.

What a special day! When we got home, we had some delicious fish for lunch. That's what most people in the country have for lunch on Palm Sunday.

DAY 3. HOLY MONDAY (MEGALI THEFTERA)

Our priests say that we remember how important it is to change our ways on this day. On Holy Monday, the godparents give their godchildren their long-awaited Easter gifts. The most special is the lampada or Easter candle, which we light at church on the night of Holy Saturday. Those who live far always make sure to send the lampades to their godchildren on time for Holy Saturday.

In honour of our godparents, Nona and Nono, Mum and Dad prepared a splendid Lent feast. They also gave them a basket filled with Easter treats and wine.

My baby brother went insane when he saw his lampada! I should tell you that lampades are colourful candles decorated with toys. It could be a superhero, a doll, a spacecraft- anything you can imagine. I got a blue scooter with lights! George got a watch with lasers, and John got a car that transforms into a shark. How cool is that? We also got colossal chocolate eggs, fantastic new trainers, and new clothes.

DAY 4. HOLY TUESDAY (MEGALI TRITI)

In this morning's service, we learned about peace and happiness from the stories we read in the church. I heard some of my mom's friends talking about how they're getting ready for their families to come over for Easter.

Mum said that in big cities, houses are thoroughly cleaned, and most Easter shopping has already been done by today. In villages, the houses and the courtyards are freshly painted white. Everything seems clean and bright!

DAY 5. HOLY WEDNESDAY (MEGALI TETARTI)

During the evening service, we heard about the story of Christ having his feet rubbed with holy oil. Back then, when you had a guest, it was considered very polite to give them water in a bowl so they could wash their feet because they had just walked through the dusty streets.

The priest talked about how important it is to confess your sins, repent, and forgive people who have hurt you. At the end of the service, we were given Holy Unction, similar to the holy oil in Christ's story. Many people believe that if you rub it on your skin, it will heal any injury you might have.

DAY 6. MAUNDY THURSDAY (MEGALI PEMPTI)

Thursday morning is when we boil and dye our eggs. Easter eggs are traditionally dyed red to represent the blood of Christ, whose resurrection is celebrated on Saturday.

Yiayia's advice for making flawless hard-boiled eggs is: Make sure the eggs are at room temperature for at least two hours before cooking them.

We also made the Easter tsoureki. Think of it like a brioche. Made with flour, milk, butter, and sugar, it's the best sweet holiday bread. It is flavoured with orange peel, mastic resin, and mahlab. But since it contains butter and milk, I'll have to wait until after church on Saturday night to try any.

Holy Thursday is the day of the Last Supper. It is called this because it was the last time Christ had dinner with his students (his apostles) before he died. He said some things at this dinner that were really important. He told them he would die but then be resurrected so all could live forever with him in heaven!

The stories at tonight's evening service focused on Christ's final instructions to his followers. The priests then carried a wooden cross into the church's centre. Next, they chanted, "Today is hung upon the Tree, he who hung the land in the midst of the waters". After that, they imitated the crucifixion of Christ using a wooden figure. The hammer's sharp sound was loud and clear.

We didn't go home after the service, much to our surprise. Instead, we stayed in the church with many more children and women to decorate the Epitaphios with bright, fresh flowers until the early hours of the morning. Epitaphios is a wooden bier that looks like a tomb. Mum explained that the top part of Epitaphios represented the sky, while the middle part represented the earth.

We had a great time staying up late! I wish you could smell the lovely flowers!

DAY 7. GOOD FRIDAY (MEGALI PARASKEVI)

Good Friday is a national holiday with schools and most businesses closed. The bells chime several times throughout the day in honour of Christ's crucifixion. It is a day of mourning, repentance, and fasting. With his burial on this day, Christ's Passion comes to an end.

Today we went to Panayia Xenia, a beautiful church at the top of a mountain on the outskirts of Volos. Mary, Jesus' mother, is referred to as Panayia in Greek. "Above all saints" is the meaning of her name. There were three crosses with wooden figures on them. Christ hung on the middle cross, and on the other crosses hung two thieves, just like thousands of years ago.

The priest climbed up a ladder and removed the wooden figure of Christ from the Cross. He then carried him inside the church and wrapped him in a white sheet. There are not many rituals similar to this. I feel incredibly fortunate to have seen it.

In the afternoon, we went to a church close to our house. It was much different from the previous days. First, the priest chanted while holding a beautiful beaded cloth. This holy fabric, according to Dad, is only used on this particular day. On it, there was the image of Christ's body, his mother, and his friends. The cloth was then placed inside the Epitaphios, which had been decorated the night before. The Epitaphios was then carried by men, and the people formed a solemn procession. We followed as well, holding our brown candles and chanting psalms.

In big towns, the Epitaphios procession circles several neighbourhoods, but in rural places, it circles the entire village. In Volos, four of the biggest churches come together to share one huge Epitaphios procession. Hundreds of people march up to the dock, displaying this magnificent sight for all to see.

When the Epitaphios returned to the church, people lined up and passed under it. It's considered a blessing.

DAY 8. HOLY SATURDAY (MEGALO SAVATO)

On Holy Saturday, the church celebrates Christ's resurrection at midnight. Everyone is happy on that day! Adults carry white candles to evening mass while children hold their lampades. The candles are then lit by the Holy Light, which is passed to the people from the priest's candle.

The Holy Light is flown in directly from Jerusalem, guarded by Orthodox priests and government leaders. It arrives in Athens early in the morning and is then distributed throughout the country in time for the midnight service.

So, we went to church all dressed up. At midnight, the priest announced, "Christos Anesti" (Christ has risen) with bells ringing and fireworks lighting up the night sky. We all kissed, hugged, and said "Christos Anesti"; the answer was "Alithos Anesti" (He has truly risen). Then, we lit our marvellous lampades and sang 'Christos Anesti' three times.

We returned home with our lit candles for the special 'resurrection' dinner. Before entering our home, Papous formed a cross with his candle flame directly beneath the door head.

MAGIRITSA SOUP

Magiritsa is a soup made from lamb offal, rice, and romaine lettuce. With this dish, the Lent fast comes to an end. Yiayia makes the world's best magiritsa!

Nona's tip for a delicious Magiritsa: Finish it with an egg-lemon sauce (Avgolemono).

TSOUGRISMA

The tradition of tsougrisma, or cracking of eggs, takes place on Holy Saturday night and Easter Sunday. This is a fun game for everyone. The cracked eggs symbolise the resurrection of Christ.

All you need to do is follow a simple set of rules. Each person picks an egg, says "Christos Anesti," and cracks it on top of another's egg while they reply, "Alithos Anesti ." Whoever gets a broken egg loses. The game continues until there is only one winner. It is believed that whoever comes out of it unscathed will have a good year ahead.

Tip for a winning egg shared by Nono: Choose a pointy egg and rub it between your hands to bring it to body temperature. This way, it's less likely to break.

DAY 9. EASTER SUNDAY (KIRIAKI TOU PASCHA)

Easter dinner is a feast for the eyes and the senses. Roasted lamb and kokoretsi are classic dishes. The men in our family came together the day before to wash and skewer the lamb and the kokoretsi. Of course, we got to help too! Kokoretsi consists of lamb intestines wrapped around seasoned offal, including lungs, kidneys, and hearts. It is not to everyone's taste, but our family loves it!

The lamb and kokoretsi were set on the spit over a charcoal burner (souvla) and slowly grilled for hours on Sunday morning. We took turns whirling the rod over the fire, which was amazing! Even our little brother helped!

Thea said that not all Greeks cook the lamb in the same way. Some cook their roasts in the oven. In Crete, they use the "antikristo" method, which means "across the fire". People there slowly cook lamb pieces on large wooden skewers in a circular formation around the fire. Sometimes it takes up to six hours to cook!

Tips for a great roast lamb and kokoretsi: Papou says, "Place lemon peels and garlic cloves in the lamb's inside. "He also adds, "While on the souvla, regularly brush the outer side with olive oil and lemon dressing."

The women in our family prepared the side dishes. Spinach pie, cheese pie, roasted potatoes with mustard and rosemary, Greek salad, horta, tzatziki, melitzanosalata, and fruits were some of them. Tsoureki, galaktoboureko and orange tart were also excellent dessert options for the day.